Over 75 Reasons We Should Have Elected Hillary Clinton as President Of the United States

Credentials a President Should Have

By Paula C. Henderson

ISBN-13: 978-1979562492

ISBN-10: 1979562490

DEDICATION

I want to dedicate this to Hillary Clinton. For all the good works. For all the sacrifices and injustices endured in order to stay the course to help the people of the United States. Even those who are against her. She perseveres. May this be an example of how we can inspire others.

CONTENTS

1 HILLARY RODHAM CLINTON

As you read through this impressive resume and background I hope you will be mindful of all the experience and wisdom one retains when involved so deeply in the job positions held, the programs, institutions and organizations as she has consistently been throughout her astounding career.

We should expect this in our President. The Presidency should not be taken lightly. Our country is not a joke and it is not trivial. It is vital we always elect someone who has the kind of experience, education and unselfish pursuits one can only get with the kind of background of Hillary Rodham Clinton.

Read this list with forethought. Really consider each achievement and each milestone. Not many can say they have achieved so much and done so much for the people of the United States.

Please note as you read through the list that many of these were programs she wanted to implement when elected. Programs very much needed still today as we approach 2018.

This is not about hanging onto the past and crying over what we lost.

I released this as a reminder that these things are still relevant!

What was important to Hillary is still important and it is imperative we carry on.

I hope reading this inspires you.

I hope it motivates you toward making change in your own life, in your community and getting even more involved in change.

This list is important in that it can remind us on what we can focus on.

I want this to reinvigorate our efforts. Not just for the goals we seek but how we pave the road to reach those goals.

May we be successful.

May YOU be successful in each of your individual endeavors.

We should not be going forward with a sense of competition but rather as a team player where-as we want everyone to succeed.

It's an old adage but I believe we are only as great as our weakest person.

We must lift everyone. Everyone.

2 HILLARY'S RESUME

1. Her background has been consistently leading Hillary to this position as President of the United States. She was elected Senior class President at Wellesley College: This is where Hillary became involved in social justice activism. After college Hillary enrolled in Yale Law School. She was one of just 27 women in her graduating class at the time.

2. Hillary graduated with honors at Yale. During law school, Hillary spent her summer researching the education and health of migrant farmworkers and their kids.

3. Hillary worked on Presidential campaigns for Barry Goldwater, George McGovern, and Jimmy Carter.

4. She co-founded the Arkansas Advocates for Children and Families

5. Hillary was the first female associate and first female partner at Rose Law Firm.

6. Named one of the 100 most powerful lawyers in America by the National Law Journal in 1988 and again in 1991.

7. Chaired the Arkansas Educational Standards Committee

8. First Lady of the United States for eight years. Don't underestimate this role. A first lady can certainly choose to not be very involved and choose to be a support only to her husband but Hillary Clinton was a very active and respectful First Lady.

9. Served as U.S. Senator from New York State from 2001-2009. Great experience!

10. She served on five (5) Senate Committees while a New York Senator: 1) Budget Committee 2) Armed Services 3) Aging 4) Environment 5) Public Works, Health Education, Labor and Pensions Committee

11. She was also a Commissioner on the Commission on Security and Cooperation in Europe

12. Served as our United States Secretary of State

13. One of Secretary Clintons greatest achievements is the Global Health Initiative also known as GHI, introduced in 2010.

14. She is Pro Equal Rights for the LGBT community

15. Hillary understands economic inequality and wants to fix it!

16. She supports Gun Control

17. She is pro-choice

18. She knows the Criminal Justice System in this country is broken and wants to be pro-active in correcting this.

19. Hillary wants to protect the Affordable Care Act and improve upon it. Not repeal it.

20. Hillary understands that Climate Change is real and takes it seriously.

21. She supports diminishing Iranian nuclear weapons through a negotiated process of inspections.

22. Supports overturning Citizens United

23. Believes we should nominate Justices to the Supreme Court who protect women's reproductive rights, continued belief in separation of church and state, supports sensible gun laws and supports EPA regulation on carbon emissions to combat climate change.

24. Opposes torture.

25. Opposes unconstitutional government surveillance on American citizens.

26. Supports raising the minimum wage to above the poverty line.

27. Hillary supports public schools.

28. Hillary wants to work toward taking out ISIS's stronghold in Iraq and Syria

29. Hillary wants to provide every student an opportunity to learn computer science.

30. Reform our criminal justice systems sentencing laws and policies and work toward ending racial profiling by law enforcement.

31. Believes in protecting the right to vote by working to mend the Voting Rights Act

32. Protect immigrant's' right's. Keeping families together. End family detention and private immigrant detention centers.

33. Hillary want to reduce air pollution, invest in the removal of toxins, develop greener and more resilient infrastructure, and encourage efforts to clean up toxic sites.

34. Hillary wants to double America's investment in Early Head Start.

35. Started a legal aid clinic in Arkansas so that low income people had access to legal representation. Helped start a program to help low income parents prepare their kids for school, which is now in more than 20 states and helped to found the Arkansas Single Parent Scholarship Fund, which helps nearly 40,000 single parents with their education.

36. Helped to pass the Children's Health Insurance Program (CHIP), now covering more than 7,000,000 kids and advocated for the expansion of Medicaid for foster kids until they are 21 years old.

37. Hillary's plan against drug addiction: Treatment and recovery; substance abuse disorders are chronic diseases and recover is only possible through effective and ongoing care – not neglect or stigmatization.

38. Providing tax relief for the smallest businesses.

39. Making sure small businesses get paid with a plan to crack down on big businesses that repeatedly stiff small businesses when the bill comes due – and to give small businesses recourse to fight back. (In light of the current president; let's all take a moment to re-read this one!)

40. Supporting small business owners and entrepreneurs. Hillary will work to provide incubators, mentoring, and training to 50,000 entrepreneurs and small business owners in underserved communities across the country. (this is something Hillary would have given us as President!)

41. Hillary is against privatizing Social Security.

42. Hillary wants Medicare to be able to negotiate lower drug prices so we have lower costs for seniors.

43. Public college or universities in state should be attainable to all students without incurring debt. (So important!)

44. Borrowers will be able to refinance loans at current rates, providing debt relief to an estimated 25 million people. They'll never have to pay back more than 10 percent of their income, and all remaining college debt will be forgiven after 20 years.

45. Delinquent school loan borrowers and those in default will get help to protect their credit and get back on their feet.

46. Strengthen American trade enforcement so we stand up to foreign countries that aren't playing by the rules.

47. Hillary is against deals like the Trans-Pacific Partnership

48. Get manufacturing back in the hardest hit communities by creating tax incentives.

49. Crack down on companies that ship jobs and earnings overseas and create incentives for companies to bring back jobs to the United States.

50. Protect wildlife by keeping Public Lands public and making more resources available to farmers, ranchers and forest landowners who are taking steps to conserve our wildlife, lands and waters.

51. Supports the Preventing Animal Cruelty and Torture Act also known as PACT

52. Restore collective bargaining rights for unions and defend against partisan attacks on workers' rights.

53. Place an exit tax on businesses that move operations overseas.

54. Accessible training programs and resources that are up to date for the 21st century technology and that lead to good jobs and lifelong skills and credentials.

55. For employers, Hillary's plan at the time of her campaign encourages businesses to invest in their workers for the long term through training, apprenticeships and creating good jobs.

56. Launch our countries boldest investment infrastructure since the construction of our interstate highway system in the 1950's.

57. Advance our commitment to research and technology in order to create the industries and jobs of the future.

58. Establish the U.S. as the clean energy superpower of the world. Her plan would include half a billion solar panels installed by the end of her first term and enough clean, renewable energy to power every home in America within 10 years of her taking office. (How exciting would this be?)

59. Strengthen American manufacturing with a $10 billion "Make it in America" plan.

60. Cut red tape! Provide tax relief and expand access to capital so small businesses can grow, hire and thrive.

61. Pursue trade policies that put U.S. job creation first.

62. Current law allows banks to invest billions through hedge funds, which are exempt from his rule. Hillary believes this loophole should be closed.

63. Hold senior bankers accountable when a large bank suffers major losses.

64. Give regulators more authority to force complex or risky firms to reorganize, downsize or break apart.

65. Extend the statute of limitations for prosecuting major financial fraud.

66. When corporations pay large fines to the government for violating the law, Hillary thinks those fines should impact the bonuses of the executives responsible at the time and it should impact their standing with the company. All in a negative way of course.

67. Holding corporations accountable when they break the law. (This should be a no brainer; ....and yet.)

68. Stick with our allies! Hillary KNOWS that NATO is one of the best investments that America has ever made.

69. She knows that diplomacy is often the only way to avoid a conflict.

70. Building stronger ties between Cuba and the United States while continuing to press for reforms.

71. She will say no to trade deals like Trans-Pacific.

72. Hillary wants to create an environment where companies invest in and shares profits with their employees! Further, she wants to crack down on companies that take profits overseas in order to avoid paying taxes.

73. Expects businesses that export jobs to give back the tax breaks they have received.

74. Hillary will fight for equal pay for women and guarantee paid leave.

75. Protect social security.

76. Overturn citizens United

77. She will ask for an SEC rule requiring publicly traded companies disclose political spending

78. Expand the New Markets Tax Credit

79. Increase funding to support family farms.

80. A commitment to clean energy.

81. Hillary will increase funds for Early Head Start, universal pre-K, and community college.

82. Hillary co-founded Arkansas Advocates for Children and Families in 1977. One of the state's first child advocacy groups.

83. At the United Nations Fourth World Conference on Women in Beijing Hillary spoke boldly about human rights and against abuses.

84. After September 11, 2001 Hillary was involved in providing healthcare for the responders who worked at ground zero.

85. Hillary worked to broaden TRICARE

86. Fights for rural areas that need access to broadband, fresh foods and other services and products the rest of us take for granted.

87. Hillary visited over 100 countries as Secretary of State. She understands the global conversation needed for diplomacy.

88. She helped to negotiate a ceasefire between Israel and Hamas that averted a war.

89. A part of the fight for a United Nations Security Council resolution concerning sexual violence against women and children in conflict zones.

90. Hillary believes America does best when the economy works for everybody, not just those at the top!

Over 75 Reasons We Should Have Elected Hillary Clinton as President Of the United States

Sources include, but are not limited to:

https://en.wikipedia.org/wiki/United_States_Senate_career_of_Hillary_Rodham_Clinton
And
www.hillaryclinton.com

3 PERSONAL COMMENTARY

Hillary lost the election. So why release this book?

Because the platform she campaigned on is still vital. We, as a people, have the power to carry on and move this country forward in the direction she envisioned and we hoped for!

I think in the past year since the election last year we have gotten lost in the anger. Our time is being taken up by arguing and fighting with our opponents.

It's time to focus. Walk away from the fighting and start DOING positive things. The positive things listed here in this book that Hillary started, founded, and campaigned on for our future.

We, of course, all have our vocations. Our "best place" to be to utilize our talents. What worries me is that many of the good works have been dropped by the waste side to be angry. Hillary's loss does not have to be in vain. She, you and I can carry on. We do not need the current administration to carry on much of this work.

The President isn't the only one who can create jobs. You and I can create jobs.

You and I can decide to pay our employees a fair and livable wage. We do not need the government to change anything for us to make those decisions as individuals, members of our communities, as neighbors and as business owners.

You and I can decide to treat people fairly.

You and I can be charitable.

You and I can decide that we will create jobs in our communities. Pay our taxes. Obey the laws. Hold others accountable for wrongdoing and you and I can go out and vote at each and every election whether it be local, state or federal elections.

You and I have a voice. We have a right to be heard.

You and I are so much more than the current administration.

This country is who YOU are. Who do you decide to be today?

You and I define this country by our decisions and actions or lack of action.

I want you to imagine you are on a road. A path. You are doing your work along the way and your good deeds. If you stop every time someone insults you, takes aim at you, yells at you; if you stop to argue with them every time they show up you and I are allowing them to slow us down to getting to our goal. Move forward and don't stop.

Gather like-minded people along the way.

In this your group you and your agendas will grow. And grow!

You don't grow your group by spending time arguing with the enemy. You grow your group by surrounding yourself by the people who have the same goals as YOU.

Then your work becomes easier and potentially more successful as you gain more and more like-minded people along this path.

One thing I have learned about the people in this country:

They want to go along with the largest group. They want to be on the winning team.

There have been surveys where people admit they vote for the person they think will win. Not who they want to vote for.

Why? Because they don't do the research and don't know who they want to vote for. Let's be fair though, politics can be complicated and politicians don't have the best track record for being honest. Many people have no idea who to believe and I think we can understand that. So, they vote for who they think will win because they want to say they were a part of the winning team. Or, they vote for who their family says they support or who their church or peers support. But honestly, there are many who simply do not know who they would vote for were it not for these guides.

With that knowledge, let's start walking a positive path and gain people as we walk toward the finish line. The win!

One person alone is not a village. A village is made up of many persons with a diverse set of skills and backgrounds in order to make it successful. This is what we are aiming for. To gather as many people on our team as we can. Not to argue with as many people as we can.

Personally I think we can be the most successful if we start with ourselves. Are we being accountable? Are we voting? Doing our part to support what we say we support. Not just in words but in action?

If you say you support small business in your community make sure you actually are supporting small businesses in your community. Being their cheerleader with positive words will not keep them afloat.

"Gosh, I hope you guys are successful" will not keep their doors open. You have to go there and buy their stuff or their services! That's what keeps them open.

After you, who is the closest people? Your family? Your co-workers? Your neighbors? Those in your local community?

Start with you and then start to expand out from there. If we all did this we would have more successful communities that were a reflection of what we believe in and support rather than the opposite.

Don't support things, ideals, businesses that do not resonate with what you think this country is about. Equality and diversity and fairness. People like to laugh at the thought of fairness. I am old enough to know life is not fair. That should not stop us from striving to make it as fair as possible.

Hire people every chance you get if you can afford that! And pay a fair wage. You don't have to be a business to help out the economy in your local area. Hire people to mow your yard, wash your windows, use the local dry cleaner and go to your local farmers markets. Pay the extra 2cents per gallon in order to keep the neighborhood gas station open instead of driving 2 miles out of your way just to save 2cents a gallon. If you do the math it just doesn't add up.

Be safe, and honor traffic laws, city ordinances, etc.

Participate in your local community. Volunteer. Donate. Care!

Vote! But vote responsibly.

Be kind. We never know what someone is going through. I have worked for employers who could care less if your mother just died. Some people have to come into work for fear of losing their jobs and have just had a life changing event take place. A cancer diagnosis at the doctor this morning before starting their shift or a sick child they cannot afford to stay home and care for.

Be kind and understand that some people have issues we know nothing about. Circumstances we know nothing about. They do not owe anyone an explanation. When I was a single mom I worked 3 jobs sometimes. I often had no choice but to shop online rather than my local stores. I lived in a small town and the stores closed at 9pm. I had a few people scold me when in casual conversation it came out I had bought something online I could have gotten in town. Hesitate before deciding to judge someone.

I don't mean to sound preachy. These are simply my own thoughts, my own aspirations that I aspire to each day. I don't always succeed. But it is what I strive for.

This past year has been challenging to say the least. At times down right scary! Right?

I want to do whatever I can to contribute to 2018 being a good year in spite of our current status as a country. Let's turn our fear and loathing, our anger and frustration into positive action.

ABOUT THE AUTHOR

Paula C. Henderson makes her home in Las Vegas, Nevada.

Paula grew up in Illinois and then moved to Ohio where, as a single mother, raised her daughter.

Becoming a certified weight loss counselor started an interest in healthy food choices and a healthy lifestyle that continues today.

Taking care of one's self is even more important when facing daily challenges. Through the years Paula has continued her education as a Nutritionist and health care advocate.

Paula has written several books on diet and nutrition. Going so far as creating a diet based on the needs of those with not just weight issues but health issues including autoimmune diseases like hypothyroidism and Rheumatoid Arthritis.

A new line of journals, day planners, countdown journals, and writing pads has been very successful this year.

Unique and varied we are sure you will find one you like. If not she also offers customization!

Visit her web site for over 50 of her publications and choose your favorite!

www.Better-U.ecwid.com

Other Published Works By Paula C. Henderson

2018 Day Planners

Black Leaf 2017-2018 Day Planner isbn: 1979348871

Owl 2017-2018 Day Planner isbn 1976028213

Cowgirl 2017-2018 Day Planner isbn 1976022282

Butterflies Fly 2017-2018 Day Planner isbn 1977678432

70 Flowers 2017-2018 Day Planner isbn 1976577284

Basic Blue 2017-2018 Day Planner isbn 1977505570

Groovy Love 2017-2018 Day Planner isbn 1975722620

Purple 2017-2018 Day Planner isbn 1974675246

Green & Gold 2017-2018 Day Planner isbn 1974670546

Horology 2017-2018 Day Planner isbn 1974645568

Blue & Silver 2017-2018 Day Planner isbn 197459341X

Balloon Rainbow 2017-2018 Day Planner isbn 1974587088

Purple Ice 2017-2018 Day Planner isbn 197458240X

Floating Hearts 2017-2018 Day Planner isbn 1974581721

B&W Dried Flower 2017-2018 Day Planner isbn 1974554376

Basic Black 2017-2018 Day Planner isbn 1974068684

Paws 2017-2018 Day Planner isbn 197572433X

Over 75 Reasons We Should Have Elected Hillary Clinton as President Of the United States

Writing Journals

Lavender Fields: a blank journal with alternating blank and lined pages ISBN-10: 1974005348

Get Well Soon A 6x9 writing journal with lined and blank pages ISBN-10: 1974185192

Deborah's Journal ISBN-10: 1548740462

Arizona: A blank journal with lines including blank pages for drawing ISBN-10: 1973804891

This Memory Book Belongs To: [your name] ISBN-10: 1973752611

Sarah's Journal: a blank journal with lines ISBN-10: 1548833339

I Claim My Joy: a blank journal with lines ISBN-10: 1548825921

May You Experience Peace: a blank journal with lines ISBN-10: 1548804665

I Trust My Instincts: a blank journal with lines ISBN-10: 1548742341

Our Thanksgiving Gratitude Journal: ruled with lines ISBN-10: 1548658715

Specialty Pads

The Music Composers Blank Sheet Music Journal: 10 Stave 100 Pages, 8.5x 11 Softback ISBN-10: 1974504409

Kitchen: A Better-U Household Notepad Series: A Better-U Household Notepad Series ISBN-10: 1974142310

Black Tie: a blank journal with lines ISBN-10: 1973863359

Warm Wishes On Your Wedding Day: a blank journal with lines ISBN-10: 1973727536

Incident Log Book: Stalking, Harassment and Domestic Abuse ISBN-10: 154501406X

My Medical Information: A Log Book ISBN-10: 1544058292

How I Got Free Stuff To Sell Online And Quit My Job: You Can Too! ISBN-10: 1542880653

Themed Pads

Be Inspired Writing Pad, Affirmations Page, Calendar and more! ISBN-10: 1974285286

Cupcake: Writing Pad, Affirmations Page, Calendar and more! ISBN-10: 1974270890

Paw Prints A 5x8 writing pad with lines: Includes: 2017/2018 Full Calendar Federal Holidays Daily Schedule Page Important Numbers & Dates ISBN-10: 1974138534

Black Tie: a blank journal with lines ISBN-10: 1973863359

Bubbles: A writing pad with lines ISBN-10: 1973864347

Shopping: lined for your lists ISBN-10: 1548898279

Write It Down Write Now ISBN-10: 1548839949

Countdown Journals

blue gradient A 90 Day Countdown Journal ISBN-10: 1977664547

90 Days To Success A 90 Day Countdown Journal ISBN-10: 1975922778 boss lady edition

Damaris 90 Days To Success: A Countdown Journal ISBN-10: 1974432432

Lynn's 90 Days To Success A Countdown Journal ISBN-10: 197433483X

Choose Healthy 90 Days To Success: a countdown journal ISBN-10: 1973997347

Angela's 90 Days To Success: A 90 Day Writing Pad With Lines. Red Edition ISBN-10: 1973949938

CEO 90 Days To Success: A 90 Day Writing Pad with Lines. Purple Edition ISBN-10: 1973947722

CEO: 90 Days To Success: a 90 day writing pad with lines ISBN-10: 1973918188

Over 75 Reasons We Should Have Elected Hillary Clinton as President Of the United States

Cookbooks

52 Low Carb Healthy Tasty Chicken Recipes: Gluten Free Dairy Free Soy Free Nightshade Free Grain Free Unprocessed, Low Carb, Healthy Ingredients:
Kindle Ed: ASIN: B0736HKLJ6
Paperback Ed: ISBN-10: 1548330884

Lettuce Amaze You: 100% Dairy, Gluten, Soy, Nightshade and Grain Free Lettuce Recipes
kindle ed: ASIN: B01N1P34BK
paperback ed: ISBN-10: 1540874931

Health Books

All You Can Eat Free Foods: A Specialty List Companion of the 5 Points Diet Plan
Kindle ed: ASIN: B01M0GHPXG

All You Can Eat Free Foods: Vegetables, Meats, Seafood and Beverages Grocery List
Paperback ed: ISBN-10: 1543155278

A Gluten and Dairy Free, Grain Free, Soy Free, and Nightshade Free Grocery List: This is "What's Left To Eat"
paperback ed: ISBN-10: 1542622727

A Gluten and Dairy Free, Grain Free, Soy Free, and Nightshade Free Grocery List
Kindle ed: ASIN: B01N7F2NQB